975.8
S

DATE DUE

APR 18

726397 50783D 03

Atlanta

Atlanta
A Downtown America Book

Pegeen Snow

D Dillon Press, Inc. Minneapolis, MN 55415

Library of Congress Cataloging-in-Publication Data

Snow, Pegeen.
    Atlanta / by Pegeen Snow.
    (A Downtown America book)
    Includes index.
    Summary: Describes the past and present, neighborhoods, historic sites, attractions, and festivals of Atlanta.
    ISBN 0-87518-389-1
    1. Atlanta (Ga.)—Juvenile literature. [1. Atlanta (Ga.)]
I. Title. II. Series.
F294.A857S64 1988
975.8'231—dc 19   88-20243
                                                  CIP
                                                  AC

ECIA-88-89

© 1988 by Dillon Press, Inc. All rights reserved

Dillon Press, Inc., 242 Portland Avenue South
Minneapolis, Minnesota 55415

Printed in the United States of America
1 2 3 4 5 6 7 8 9 10 97 96 95 94 93 92 91 90 89 88

Photographic Acknowledgments

The photographs are reproduced through the courtesy of: the Atlanta Convention and Visitors Bureau; the Center for Puppetry Arts; Steve Elmore/Tom Stack and Associates; Richard Lubrant Photography; and the Tourist Division, Georgia Department of Industry and Trade. Cover Photo by Richard Lubrant.

Contents

Fast Facts about Atlanta — 6
1 The Big Peach — 11
2 Center of the Southeast — 19
3 From Cabbagetown to Buckhead — 31
4 All Around Atlanta — 41
Places to Visit in Atlanta — 55
Atlanta: A Historical Time Line — 57
Index — 59

Fast Facts about Atlanta

Atlanta: Capital of Georgia; Fulton County seat; The Gate City; New York of the South; The Big A; The Big Peach

Location: Southeastern United States; north central Georgia

Area: City, 132 square miles (342 square kilometers); metropolitan area, 5,192 square miles (13,448 square kilometers)

Population (1986 estimate*): City, 421,910; metropolitan area, 2,560,500

Major Population Groups: Blacks, whites (mainly of English, German, Irish, and Scottish backgrounds)

Altitude: 1,010 feet (308 meters) above sea level

Climate: Average temperature is 42°F (6°C) in January, 78°F (26°C) in July; average annual precipitation is 48 inches (122 centimeters)

Founding Date: 1837, chartered as a city in 1847

City Seal: The Phoenix is shown rising from flames; date of Atlanta's incorporation (1847) is shown to the left of the Phoenix; date 1865, when Atlanta began rebuilding from Civil War, is shown to its right; Latin word *Resurgens*, meaning rising again, appears over Phoenix's head

Form of Government: Atlanta's city government is headed by a mayor. An eighteen-member city council passes laws affecting the city. Both the mayor and council are elected to four-year terms of office.

Important Industries: Airlines, aircraft manufacturing, communications, hotels and motels (hospitality industry), financial services, processed foods, forest products

*U.S. Bureau of the Census 1988 population estimates available in fall 1989; official 1990 census figures available in 1991-92.

Festivals and Parades

January: Martin Luther King Day Parade

February: Annual Children's Festival at Woodruff Arts Center

March: St. Patrick's Day Parade

April: Atlanta Dogwood Festival and Parade; Atlanta Hunt and Steeplechase; Inman Park Festival and tours

June: Atlanta Jazz Festival

July: Peachtree Road Race; Salute to America Parade; Fantastic Fourth Celebration

September: Atlanta Greek Festival; Arts Festival of Atlanta; Yellow Daisy Festival

October: Scottish Festival and Highland Games

November: Lighting of "The Great Christmas Tree" at Rich's Department Store on Thanksgiving Night

December: Christmas at Callenwolde; Peach Bowl football game and parade

For further information about festivals and parades, see agencies listed on page 56.

1

The Big Peach

Atlanta, Georgia. For some people the name brings to mind the war-torn, burning city of *Gone with the Wind*, Atlantan Margaret Mitchell's famous book about the Civil War. For others, the name Atlanta brings thoughts of a colorful, flower-filled springtime, dense, shady trees, and beautiful homes. For still others, the name suggests skyscrapers, big stores, and exciting music, dance, and plays.

All these pictures are accurate. Atlanta was the scene of some important Civil War battles before it was burned to the ground by Union troops. Each spring, Atlanta is a wonderland of color when the dogwoods, redbuds, and azaleas bloom in its tree-filled parks and neighborhoods. In parts of Atlanta there are large, elegant homes that look as if they could have been plantation houses in the Old South.

Atlanta's downtown skyline rises above the rolling hills of the Piedmont Plateau.

Atlanta is also a fast-paced, modern city with tall buildings designed in many shapes and styles. It has fine stores and shopping malls, museums, a symphony orchestra, a botanical garden, dance companies, a zoo, and theaters presenting many kinds of plays. It also has professional baseball, football, and basketball, and an international airport.

In short, Atlanta is an interesting blend of the past and the present, the natural and the manufactured. It is a place where bronze plaques marking Civil War battle sites can be found near gleaming glass office towers. It is also a place where red-tailed hawks can be seen soaring over quiet, wooded neighborhoods near some of the busiest streets in the Southeast.

Atlanta is the capital of Georgia. It is located in the north central part of the state, about fifty miles (eighty kilometers) south of the southern end of the Appalachian Mountain chain. The city lies on the Piedmont Plateau, which is a region of red clay soil and gently rolling hills.

Because of its nearness to the mountains, Atlanta has an elevation of 1,010 feet (308 meters). This high elevation saves the city from much of the summer heat that broils other parts of Georgia. But the elevation can sometimes cause problems in the winter—which in Atlanta means January and February. Then a drop of a degree or two in temperature can change a normal rainstorm into a dreaded ice storm. In such a storm, freezing rain coats and breaks tree limbs and power lines and glazes roads. One joke around the city is that the best way to scare an Atlantan is with the words, "Ice storm's coming!"

A good place from which to see all of Atlanta, and everything for fifty miles around, is atop the Westin Peachtree Plaza Hotel in downtown Atlanta. At seventy-three stories, the Peachtree Plaza is the tallest hotel in North America. From inside its revolving rooftop restaurant, people can see the airplanes coming and going from Hartsfield International Airport far to the south, the gold-domed capitol building downtown, and the huge granite rock formation called Stone Mountain east of the city. On a clear day, they can even see all the way

The sleek Westin Peachtree Plaza Hotel towers over Atlanta.

It's hard to go anywhere in Atlanta without seeing the name *Peachtree*.

north to the Appalachian Mountains and west into Alabama.

The Peachtree Plaza Hotel is located on Peachtree Street, Atlanta's main street. To many confused visitors, it seems that Atlantans cannot think of any name other than Peachtree for their streets! There are Peachtree Battle, Peachtree Circle, Peachtree Avenue, Peachtree Drive, Peachtree Place—seventeen Peachtrees within Atlanta's city limits, and nearly fifty within the metropolitan area.

It is somewhat surprising that

Peachtree is such a popular name in Atlanta. Although Georgia is known for its peaches, the fruit grows far south of Atlanta in the central part of the state. One legend says the name came into use because of a large (and rare) peach tree that grew near the spot where Atlanta was founded. Another story claims it is based on the Creek Indian word for pitch tree, or pine tree. However it happened, the name Peachtree has taken root in Atlanta and is thriving.

Even without peach trees, Atlanta has a great deal of natural beauty. Parks, both large and small, are scattered throughout the city. One of the best known is Piedmont Park, which is the site of many community events.

Atlanta's beautiful parks, pleasant climate, many things to see and do, job opportunities, and eagerness for new business all attract people and companies to the city. Many Atlantans work for companies that offer assistance or services, such as the hotels and restaurants that help make Atlanta the third-largest convention center in America.

Atlanta also has many teachers, doctors, police and firefighters, bus drivers, and workers who clean up the city and keep it in good repair. Because the Atlanta area is growing so fast, people with many different skills are needed to help build offices, homes, freeways, and MARTA (Metropolitan Atlanta Rapid Transit Authority), the city's sleek rapid rail system.

A MARTA train speeds through the city.

Some people call Atlanta the New York of the South, but Atlantans are more likely to call their city the Big Peach. If asked why, they may reply that the name Peachtree is everywhere in Atlanta. Or they may answer that a peach is a good symbol for the biggest city in Georgia. Then again, they may say that Atlanta is a peach of a place to live.

Located not far from downtown, Piedmont Park is the site of many outdoor events.

Center of the Southeast

Atlanta's location is the reason there is an Atlanta. The city lies at the center of the Southeast. Highways, rail lines, and air routes extend from it like spokes from a wheel, making it a major hub for travel and business.

It all began with railroads. In 1837, the Western and Atlantic Railroad wanted to run a rail line from Tennessee into north central Georgia. A surveyor decided the area around present-day Atlanta was the ideal spot to end the new line. He drove a stake into the ground to mark the end, or terminus, of the railroad. This stake also marked the beginning of a new town called Terminus.

At first Terminus was little more than a dot on a map, but soon it became the meeting point for three major railroads. In 1843, its name was changed to Marthasville, in hon-

Reminders of Atlanta's Civil War past are visible throughout the city.

or of the daughter of a Georgia governor. Two years later, the community's name became Atlanta, probably from the word *Atlantic* in Western and Atlantic Railroad.

During the Civil War, Atlanta's railroads made the city a major supply center for the Confederate states. When Union forces set out to break Confederate supply lines, Atlanta became an important military target. In September 1864, after a long and bloody struggle, Atlanta surrendered to the Union army's General William T. Sherman. Sherman ordered his troops to remove Atlanta's citizens and burn the city before they pushed on toward Savannah. It looked like the end of the line for the little railroad community.

Soon after Sherman's troops marched away, however, many people returned to Atlanta. These people were determined to build a bigger and better city on the ashes of the old. They immediately set to work to rebuild Atlanta into a transportation and commercial, or business, center. Rail lines were repaired, old businesses were reopened, new businesses were started, and Atlanta's population rapidly grew. In 1868, just four years after Sherman's troops destroyed the city, Atlanta became the capital of Georgia.

That same year, the *Atlanta Constitution*, one of the city's two major newspapers, was founded. The *Constitution* grew in importance during the 1880s, when Henry Grady was the

The Cyclorama, a huge painting in Grant Park, shows the hard-fought Battle of Atlanta.

paper's managing editor. Grady was the leading spokesman for the New South. This movement encouraged southern states to rebuild their businesses and create new ones. Grady worked to convince northern businessmen to invest in opportunities in the South. Through his editorials in the *Constitution* and speeches presented all over the United States. Grady urged the South to rise to the challenge of progress.

Under Grady's leadership, Atlanta became the center of the New South movement. The city attracted business interests by hosting the International Cotton Exposition of 1881, the Piedmont Exhibition of 1887, and the Cotton States and International Exposition of 1895. These events turned the attention of the North, and of the world, to the opportunities for business and industry in the South, and especially Atlanta.

Today, more than four hundred major companies have offices in Atlanta, and several nationally known companies have headquarters there. Among those companies, Coca-Cola is perhaps best known to Atlantans. First sold as a medicine, Coke was invented by Atlanta pharmacist John S. Pemberton in 1886. The Lockheed-Georgia Company, which builds big military and cargo aircraft, is Atlanta's largest manufacturer. Delta Airlines has its headquarters in Atlanta, and is one of the city's largest service companies.

Big business is only one measure

of Atlanta's growth. Education is another. "I'm a Rambling Wreck from Georgia Tech" is a familiar tune around the United States. It comes from the Georgia Institute of Technology, one of several colleges and universities that have made Atlanta an educational center for the Southeast. Georgia State University, attended by more than twenty thousand students, is located in downtown Atlanta. Emory University, which has a large medical school and hospital, lies on the eastern edge of the city. Oglethorpe University, Agnes Scott College, Mercer University, and the Atlanta University Center are all located within the Atlanta metropolitan area.

Atlanta also continues to grow as a center for the performing and visual

Students in a laboratory at Georgia Tech.

arts. Under the leadership of Robert Shaw, the Atlanta Symphony Orchestra has become known around the world. The Atlanta Ballet, an outstanding regional dance company, has paved the way for the development of many kinds of dance companies in the city. The Academy and Alliance theaters are two of the best known of Atlanta's many live theater companies. And Atlanta's High Museum of Art excites visitors with both its paintings and sculptures and its modern-looking, brilliant white building.

Atlanta's increasing role as a government center is yet another measure of the city's growth. Since the Georgia state capitol building was finished in 1889, government has become one of Atlanta's leading

The High Museum of Art.

The Georgia state capitol building.

employers. The city, county (Atlanta is in Fulton County), and state governments all employ many workers.

In addition, Atlanta is a regional center for federal government services. One federal agency that has always been located in Atlanta is the Centers for Disease Control (CDC), which is part of the U.S. Public Health Service. The CDC tracks down and studies contagious diseases around the world.

Being the center of the Southeast was not enough for Atlantans. Some years ago, Atlanta leaders saw that to continue to grow, Atlanta needed business and cultural ties with the rest of the world. In the 1970s, Atlanta stated that it planned to become America's next international city. Since then, it has worked hard to meet that goal.

International air travel has opened Atlanta up to much of the world. Hartsfield International Airport challenges Chicago's O'Hare for the title of world's busiest airport. It offers nonstop flights to most major European cities, as well as to parts of Asia and Latin America. The number of the airport's international flights continues to grow.

With direct air service available, more and more foreign-owned companies are locating in Atlanta. Some have only sales offices in the city, while others have decided to make Atlanta their U.S. headquarters.

Foreign businesses in Atlanta range from manufacturing to real estate. To encourage such companies, Atlanta's business and government leaders regularly travel to other countries to encourage foreign investment in the city. In recent years, city officials have made special efforts to tell African nations about Atlanta's opportunities.

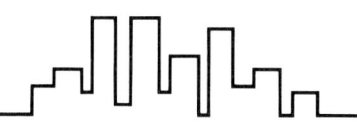

The study of international relations has grown along with Atlanta's international activities. The Carter Center of Emory University provides a setting where government and other leaders can meet to talk about issues that affect the nations of the world. The Southern Center for International Studies, located in northwest Atlanta, has several different programs in international relations.

Atlanta's international efforts have encouraged more than business. Forty-two countries now have official ties with the city. On the person-to-person level, many Atlantans take part in Friendship Force activities. The Friendship Force program was begun while Jimmy Carter was president. Its purpose is to build international friendships by helping people from around the world get to know each other. The Friendship Force sends volunteer "ambassadors" to stay in the homes of host families in other countries, and places visiting foreigners with American hosts.

Atlanta recently gained worldwide attention because of its efforts to become the site of the 1996 Summer Olympic Games. The U.S. Olympic Committee chose Atlanta to rep-

resent the United States in the process of selecting the city where the Olympics will be held. If the International Olympic Committee thinks that Atlanta would be the best choice for the sports event, then the Big Peach will host the 1996 Summer Games.

Atlanta has come a long way since Union soldiers left the city in ashes. Remembering that time, and the progress made since then, its citizens have chosen the Phoenix as the city's official symbol. This fictional bird is said to die in fire and then rise from its own ashes with renewed strength. Atlantans think that is a very good description of what their city has done.

National and world leaders come to the Carter Presidential Center to discuss global issues.

From Cabbagetown to Buckhead

At the end of the Civil War, with slavery and big plantations gone forever, large numbers of Georgians had to find new ways of life. Many, both black and white, moved to up-and-coming Atlanta to start over again. They were joined by other Southerners and even some Northerners who came to establish businesses in the city as it was being rebuilt. During the 1880s, several cotton mills opened in Atlanta. People from Appalachia and other areas came to the city to work in the mills.

As Atlanta continued to grow into a business and transportation center, it drew people from all parts of the United States. More recently, Atlanta's international interests have brought people to the city from around the world. Some foreign-born people have come to live and work in

Flowers and trees surround this home, located in one of Atlanta's wealthy neighborhoods.

Atlanta; others have come to study at its colleges and universities. Today, so many people move to Atlanta from other places that the only people hard to find in the city are native Atlantans!

Just as Atlantans come from many different places, they live in many different kinds of homes. Apartment buildings and condominiums in many styles can be found all around Atlanta—especially in the suburbs. But in many city neighborhoods, people still live in single-family houses. A look at Atlanta's neighborhoods reveals a lot about the city's history, character, and growth.

Ansley Park, which borders Piedmont Park in the heart of the city, is one of Atlanta's beautiful old neighborhoods. It is known for its winding streets and its attractive parks and gardens. Homes here range from small cottages to near-castles. The first homes in Ansley were built in 1904. In the 1970s, this area was included on the National Register of Historic Districts.

Just west of downtown Atlanta is a neighborhood called the West End. This community is older than the city itself. It was first settled in 1835, two years before Atlanta (Terminus) was founded. The West End developed as an independent city and was noted for its handsome cottages. In the late 1800s, it became part of Atlanta.

Over the years, the once-thriving neighborhood gradually fell into decay. Then in the 1960s and 1970s,

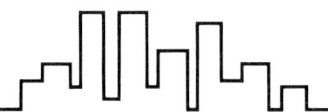

people who lived there began working to repair and restore the area's houses. Those efforts were successful, and today the West End once again has its own special look and charm.

The Wren's Nest, located on Gordon Street in the West End, was once the home of Joel Chandler Harris. Harris is best known as the author of the Uncle Remus stories, with such characters as Br'er Rabbit and Br'er Fox. The Wren's Nest has been preserved as a museum.

Also located in the West End is the Atlanta University Center, a group of several mostly black colleges. The center includes Atlanta University, Clark, Morris Brown, Spelman, and Morehouse colleges, and the Interdenominational Theological Seminary. Many outstanding black Americans, including Martin Luther King, Jr., have graduated from the schools in the Atlanta University Center. Many African leaders have also studied there.

A short distance east of downtown is one of Atlanta's most unusual neighborhoods. Really a city within a city, Cabbagetown was built in the 1880s by the Fulton Bag and Cotton Mill to house the Appalachian mountain families that were working for the company. The wood-frame dwellings of Cabbagetown are either two-story, four-family buildings or narrow, one-story homes.

Though the cotton mill closed in the early 1970s, many descendants of the first mill workers still live in

Cabbagetown. They take special pride in keeping up traditional mountain arts and crafts. And they have resisted efforts by people from outside the area to buy and make changes in neighborhood homes.

People are not sure how Cabbagetown got its unusual name. According to one story, a truck loaded with cabbages once overturned in the area. People dashed from their homes, gathered up the vegetables, and cooked them for dinner.

Also east of downtown is the neighborhood known as Inman Park. Though it is now part of Atlanta, Inman Park was the city's first suburb. Developed in the 1880s, it was connected to the city by streetcar.

Inman Park became the home of some of Atlanta's wealthiest families, who built large, beautiful homes there. Later, the area became run-down. Then in the late 1960s, Atlantans began buying its neglected old mansions and restoring them to their former greatness. Today, the people of Inman Park show their pride in the neighborhood by staging an annual festival and tour of homes.

Many of the most beautiful homes in Atlanta (and some say in America) are found in Buckhead, in the northwest part of the city. This neighborhood may have gotten its name from an early tavern where the head of a buck, a male deer, was mounted. Buckhead is made up of homes ranging in size from large to enormous. Some Buckhead homes

Candler House in Inman Park. Asa Candler was the founder of the Coca-Cola Company.

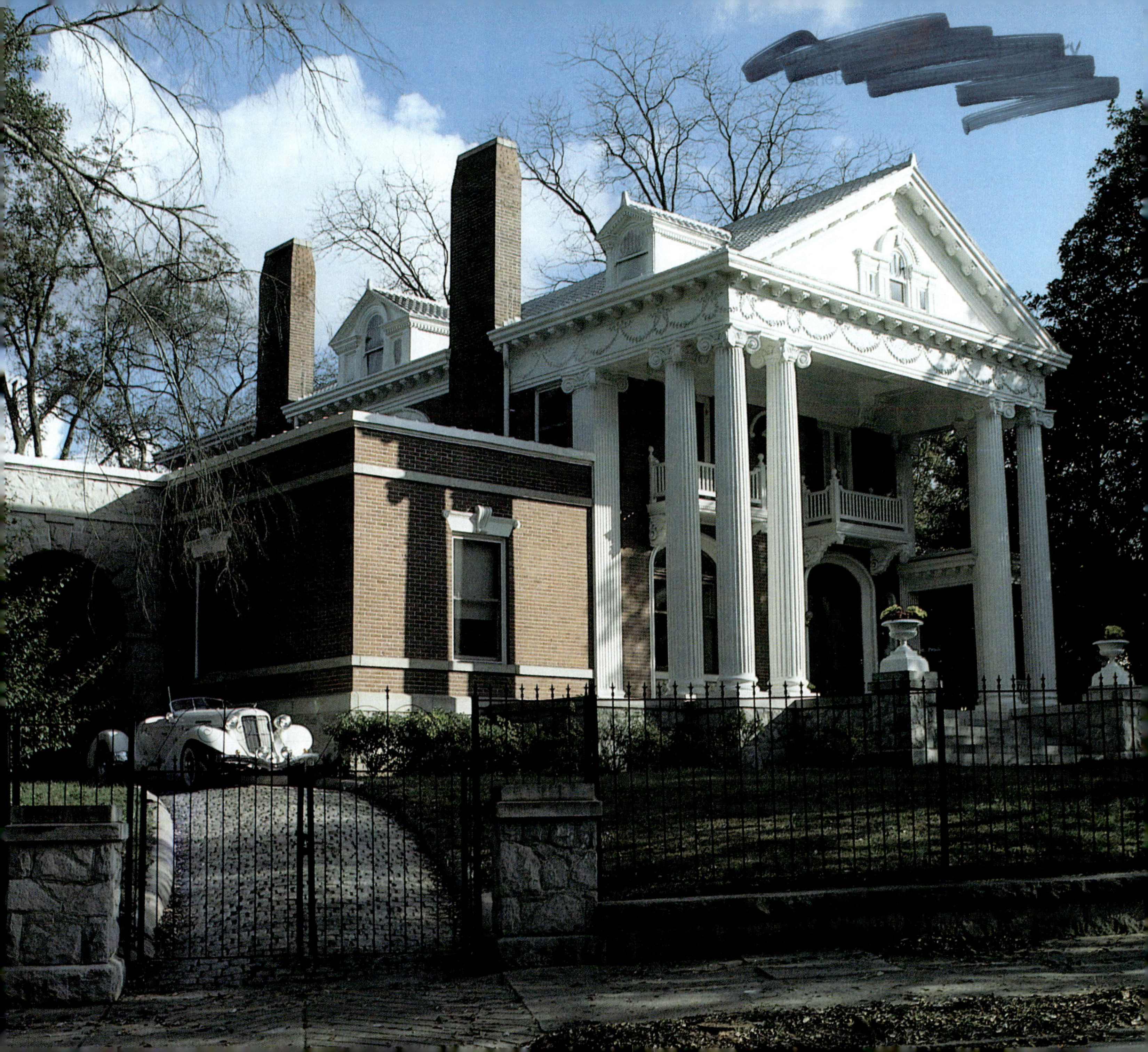

look like European villas, while others resemble old-style plantation houses. A number of these homes could even be mistaken for palaces.

Since 1967, the governor's mansion has been located in Buckhead. The white-columned, thirty-room home is found on West Paces Ferry Road. It is just one of the many beautiful houses that make a tour of Buckhead popular with visitors to Atlanta.

On the eastern edge of Atlanta's downtown business district lies Auburn Avenue, a street with a special place in Atlanta's history. "Sweet Auburn" was the center of black business and entertainment in Atlanta during the days of segregation, when blacks and whites lived and worked in separate parts of the city.

With the end of legal segregation in the 1960s, black businesses were at last able to locate anyplace in the city. As many businesses moved to other parts of town, Auburn Avenue became less important as a commercial and entertainment center.

Yet a few of Auburn's historic businesses remained, and thrive today. Among them are the Atlanta Life Insurance Company, one of the nation's major black-owned businesses, and the *Atlanta Daily World*, America's oldest black-owned newspaper. Recently, the Royal Peacock, a famous Auburn Avenue music club, was restored and reopened. This is a step toward what Atlantans, both black and white, hope will be a return of good times to Sweet Auburn.

The governor's mansion is just one of the elegant homes found in Buckhead.

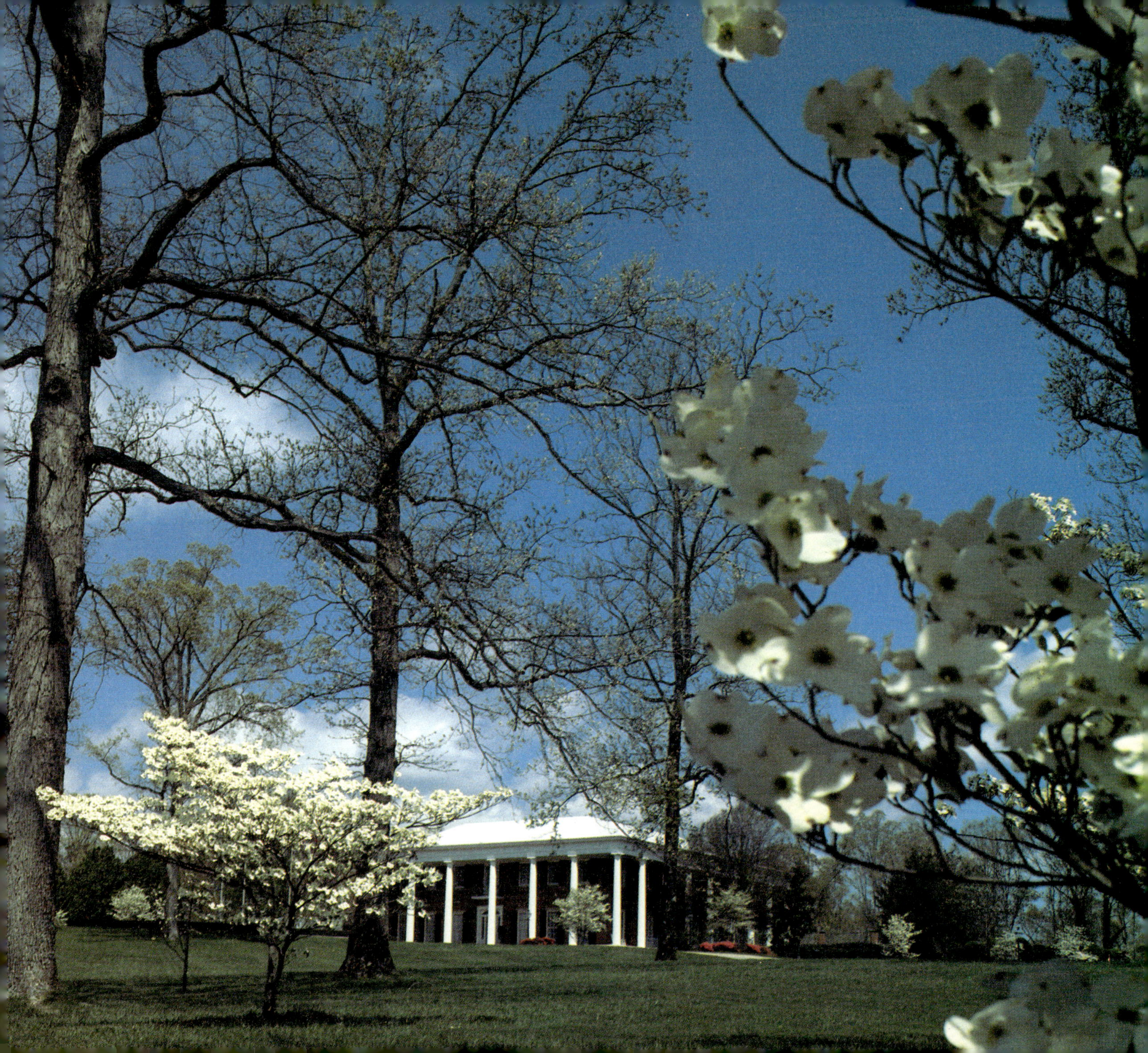

The house where Martin Luther King, Jr., was born is located on Auburn Avenue.

Auburn Avenue was also the childhood home of Dr. Martin Luther King, Jr. Dr. King was born in Atlanta in 1929, a time when segregation still separated blacks and whites throughout the South. As a minister and civil rights leader, he worked against segregation in many ways, but never through the use of violence. Dr. King's beliefs and actions helped Atlanta leaders, both black and white, bring segregation in the city to a peaceful end in the 1960s. King's work also helped Atlantans accept other black leaders; in 1973, Atlanta became the first major Southern city to elect a black mayor.

The Martin Luther King, Jr., National Historic Site and Preservation District is located on Auburn

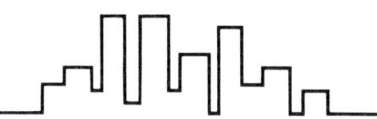

Avenue just east of the avenue's business district. It includes the Ebenezer Baptist Church, where Dr. King and his father were both pastors, and Dr. King's burial site and memorial hall. The Martin Luther King Community Center, the Martin Luther King, Jr., Center for Nonviolent Social Change, and the house where Dr. King was born are also located within the historic district.

Atlanta has so many interesting neighborhoods that even long-time residents of the city sometimes discover places they had not known about before. To Atlantans, that is one of the many things that make life in the Big Peach so exciting.

Peachtree Road Race
STAR
The Atlanta Journal
Etonic
Lite
NO

All Around Atlanta

Atlanta is full of interesting, unusual places to visit and has many activities for people of all ages. Lush, green parks, historic sites, sports events, art and music festivals—all these things attract Atlantans and visitors alike.

Atlantans enjoy the outdoors, and often take advantage of Atlanta's mild weather to get out, exercise, and have fun. Tennis, golf, and jogging are especially popular. Some city parks, including Piedmont Park, have public tennis courts, and some feature golf courses. Atlantans both young and old like to trot along the city's gentle hills, enjoying the scenery and improving their health.

The more serious runners meet on the Fourth of July for the Peachtree Road Race. Twenty-five thousand runners, ages ten and up, run down Peachtree Road from the Len-

Thousands of runners cross the starting line of the ten-kilometer Peachtree Road Race.

ox Square shopping mall in northeast Atlanta to the finish line at Piedmont Park. The race covers 6.2 miles (10 kilometers). It begins at eight in the morning so runners can avoid the midday heat. Even at that early hour, large crowds line the course to cheer on family, friends, and the world-class runners who take part in the event.

The Peachtree Junior, an offshoot of the Peachtree Road Race, is a two-mile (three-kilometer) "fun run" for children ages seven to twelve. It is held in early June on a course within Piedmont Park.

Atlantans of all ages enjoy the Chattahoochee River, which flows along and above the northern city limits. The "Hooch" is both the source of Atlanta's water and a source of outdoor fun. Whether they are canoeing, rafting, fishing, or just relaxing on the river's green banks, Atlantans appreciate the beauty of the gentle Chattahoochee.

Children and adults can get a close-up look at nature at the Fernbank Science Center. Located just east of the city in Decatur, Fernbank is run by the DeKalb County school system. One of the center's most outstanding features is a large forest preserve with trees that have been growing since long before Atlanta was founded. Other features of the center are an observatory where people can look at the stars and planets through a telescope, a planetarium with models of the universe, a museum, and a

Rafting down the Chattahoochee River is a popular pastime with Atlantans.

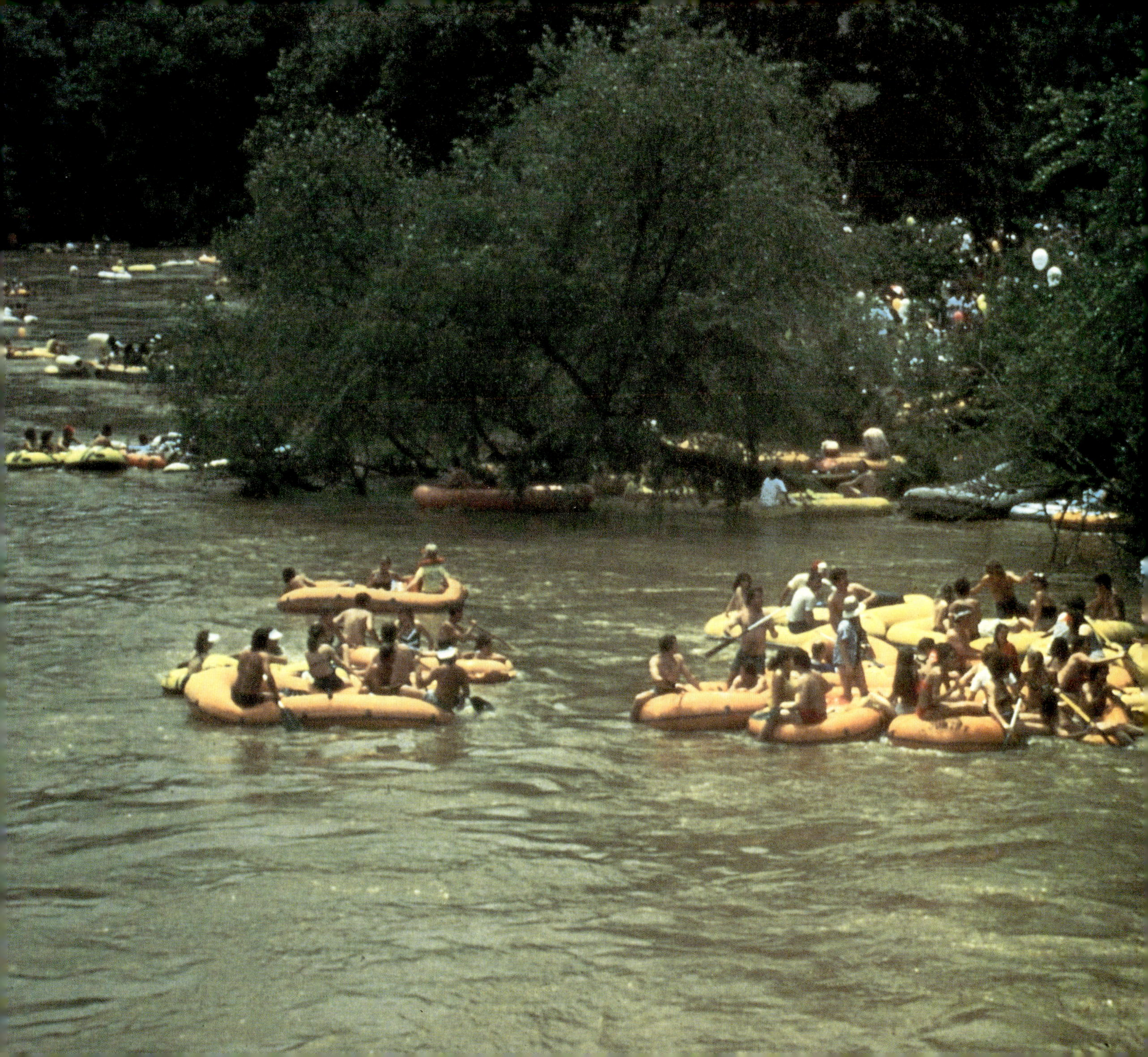

The Braves and the Falcons play at Atlanta-Fulton County Stadium.

greenhouse. Among Fernbank's most popular exhibits is the *Apollo* 6 space capsule.

Atlanta-Fulton County Stadium offers outdoor sports events almost year round. The stadium is home to the Atlanta Braves baseball team and the Atlanta Falcons football team. It was at this stadium, on April 8, 1974, that Braves slugger Henry Aaron hit his 715th home run and broke Babe Ruth's long-standing record.

A favorite place to visit for both young and old is Stone Mountain

Stone Mountain Park features train rides around the mountain.

Park, located a short distance east of Atlanta. This large park surrounds Stone Mountain, an 825-foot (252-meter) granite dome. The north face of the mountain features an enormous carving of three Confederate leaders: Jefferson Davis, Robert E. Lee, and Thomas "Stonewall" Jackson. Visitors to the park can watch a colorful laser show that uses the mountain as a backdrop. They can also visit a genuine plantation house, ride a cable car to the top of Stone Mountain, and take a tour of the park by

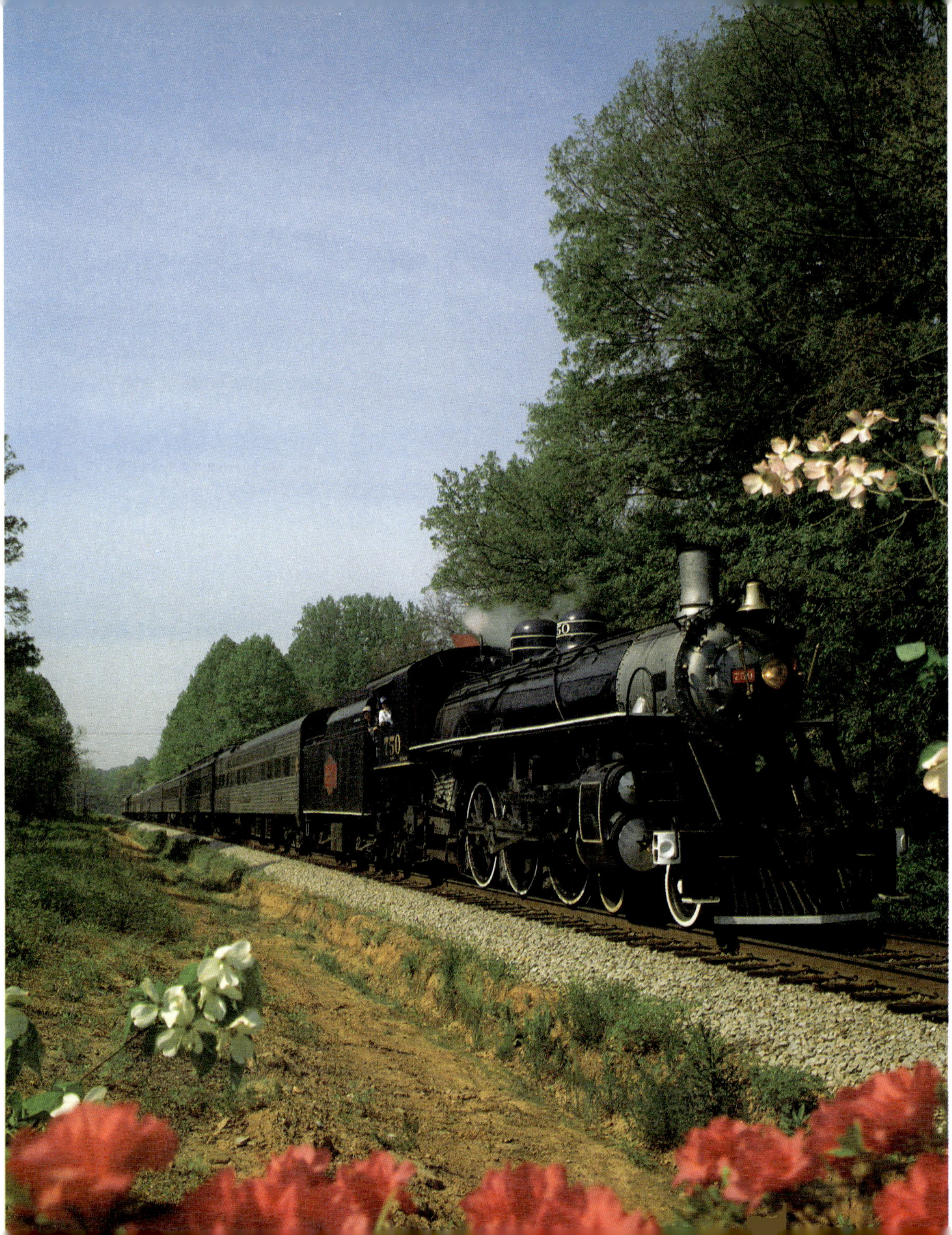
750

paddle wheel riverboat or by railroad.

Atlantans can get a sense of their city's early rail history by riding the New Georgia Railroad. Using historic steam and diesel engines and rail cars built from the 1920s to the 1950s, the railroad offers passenger trips around the Atlanta area. One route is an eighteen-mile (twenty-nine-kilometer) loop around the northern part of the city. Another runs from central Atlanta to the Stone Mountain area.

The Atlanta Cyclorama in Grant Park is a huge painting that shows the 1864 Battle of Atlanta. Lifelike carved figures added to its base make the painting appear almost real. The Cyclorama was painted in Milwaukee, Wisconsin, in the 1880s. It changed owners several times and was exhibited in a number of cities around the country. In the early 1890s, it was purchased by a Georgia businessman and put on display in Grant Park. Several years later, the painting was donated to the city for generations of Atlantans to admire.

Atlantans can enjoy a taste of the South at the Atlanta State Farmers Market. Here visitors find all the traditional fruits and vegetables for which the South is noted. This is the largest of several big Atlanta markets selling such Southern favorites as black-eyed peas, collards, mustard and turnip greens, sweet potatoes, okra, and yellow squash. Located just south of the city, its acres of long produce sheds offer everything from Georgia peaches to Georgia onions.

Restored engines and passenger cars on the New Georgia Railroad offer scenic tours of Atlanta.

Almost every month brings a special event celebrating something about Atlanta or its people. The year begins with a celebration of Martin Luther King Day. On the third Monday in January, Atlantans turn out for a big parade that begins downtown on Peachtree Street and ends at the King Center on Auburn Avenue. Later, many national and world leaders attend a special service at the Ebenezer Baptist Church.

Each April, Atlanta looks as if it has been hit by a pink-and-white blizzard when its thousands of dogwood trees bloom. The Atlanta Dogwood Festival is a nine-day celebration of the city's favorite tree. Many events take place during the festival, including a colorful parade, garden tours, and a hot-air balloon race at Piedmont Park.

September is the time of the Atlanta Greek Festival, which is held at the Greek Orthodox Cathedral of the Annunciation. During this popular four-day festival, Atlantans of Greek heritage celebrate their traditions with music, dancing, exhibits, and delicious food. Children as young as six take part in traditional Greek dances. Young people especially like to sample Greek desserts, such as the honey-drenched pastry called baklava.

In October, the Scottish Festival and Highland Games are held at Stone Mountain Park. This event is popular with Atlantans of many national backgrounds. People of Scottish ancestry come to watch or take

Scottish pipers march in a parade during the Scottish Festival and Highland Games.

part in traditional highland games. Visitors flock to a contest in which strong men hurl a tree trunk called a caber. Folk dancing, Scottish foods, crafts, and music are also part of the festivities.

There are many opportunities to enjoy the arts in Atlanta, including two major festivals. In either February or March, the Children's Festival is held at the Woodruff Arts Center. This event brings children together to get to know and enjoy the city's performing and visual arts. It includes

The Arts Festival features everything from hand-stitched quilts to symphony music.

many kinds of music and dance, plus visual art, plays, puppetry, and special workshops.

In September, Piedmont Park is the site of the Arts Festival of Atlanta, one of the city's most popular outdoor events. The Arts Festival features many kinds of visual and performing arts. A number of programs and activities are designed especially for young people. They include performances by members of the Atlanta Symphony Orchestra and Atlanta Opera, puppet shows, and entertainment by clowns and magicians. In the festival's workshops, children learn to make such things as puppets and collages, and even learn how to juggle. A children's sand-sculpting contest adds to the fun.

During the rest of the year, Atlanta's young people can take part in a wide range of activities offered by the city's performing arts programs. The Atlanta Symphony Orchestra has two series of children's concerts. Symphony Street concerts, intended for younger children, are given at seven Atlanta locations. These performances present short musical works by several different classical composers. They are made especially lively by the use of dancers, many special props, and narration, or a spoken storyline. Young People's Concerts for older children are performed at Symphony Hall in the Woodruff Arts Center. These narrated concerts present works by composers such as Mozart, Beethoven, and Bartok, and sometimes include performances by singers and dancers.

The Atlanta Children's Theatre, which is part of the Alliance Theatre, presents a fall and spring play each year. These plays are performed at the Alliance Theatre in Atlanta and also at a number of locations around Georgia.

The Academy Theatre in midtown Atlanta presents various plays for children. Many Atlanta families return each year for its annual production of *A Christmas Carol*.

Young Atlantans show the puppets they have made at the Center for Puppetry Arts.

The Center for Puppetry Arts helps Atlantans of all ages to appreciate puppetry as a highly developed art form. Located in central Atlanta, it offers one series of performances for children and another for adults. The center also has a school of puppetry where children and adults can learn to design and build their own puppets. In addition, the center operates a puppetry museum and holds a summer festival and touring program.

Through its art programs, parks, and special events, Atlanta has much to offer. It is a city of historical interest and natural beauty. It is also a city of big buildings and big businesses—and big plans for the future.

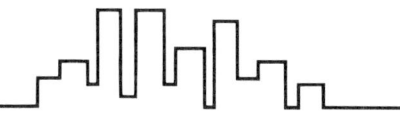

A popular saying among Atlantans is that once people live in Atlanta, they never leave. Some people do leave, of course, but Atlanta's style and spirit stay with them wherever they go.

Places to Visit in Atlanta

Academy Theatre
173 14th Street NE
(404) 892-0880

Alliance Theatre Company
Woodruff Arts Center
1280 Peachtree Street NE
(404) 892-2414

Atlanta Botanical Gardens
1345 Piedmont Avenue NE
(404) 876-5858

Atlanta Children's Theatre
Woodruff Arts Center
1280 Peachtree Street NE
(404) 892-2414

Atlanta-Fulton County Stadium
521 Capitol Avenue SE
(404) 522-7630

Atlanta Municipal Market
209 Edgewood Avenue SE
(404) 659-1665

Atlanta State Farmers Market
16 Forest Parkway, Forest Park
(404) 366-6910

Callenwolde Fine Arts Center
980 Briarcliff Road NW
(404) 872-5338

Carter Presidential Center
1 Copenhill Avenue NE
(404) 523-7631

Center for Puppetry Arts
1404 Spring Street
(404) 873-3391

Chattahoochee Nature Center
9135 Willeo Road, Roswell
(404) 992-2055

Fernbank Science Center
156 Heaton Park Drive NE, Decatur
(404) 378-4311

High Museum of Art
Woodruff Arts Center
1280 Peachtree Street NE
(404) 892-4444

Martin Luther King, Jr., Center for Nonviolent Social Change
449 Auburn Avenue NE
(404) 524-1956

Martin Luther King, Jr., National Historic Site and Preservation District
Auburn Avenue, between Jackson and Randolph streets
(404) 331-3919

Six Flags Over Georgia
7561 Six Flags Road SE, Austell
(404) 739-3400
Amusement park

Stone Mountain Park
Highway 78 East, Stone Mountain
(404) 498-5600

Woodruff Arts Center
1280 Peachtree Street NE
(404) 892-3600
Includes Atlanta Symphony Orchestra, Alliance Theatre Company, Atlanta Children's Theatre, Atlanta Opera, Atlanta College of Art, and High Museum of Art

Wren's Nest
1050 Gordon Street SW
(404) 753-8535

Zoo Atlanta
800 Cherokee Avenue SE
(404) 624-5678

Additional information can be obtained from these agencies:

Atlanta Chamber of Commerce
235 International Boulevard NW
Atlanta, Georgia 30301
(404) 586-8400

Atlanta Convention and Visitors Bureau
233 Peachtree Street NE
Atlanta, Georgia 30303
(404) 521-6600

Atlanta Historical Society
3101 Andrews Drive NW
Atlanta, Georgia 30305
(404) 261-1837

National Park Service
75 Spring Street SW
Atlanta, Georgia 30303
(404) 331-5187

Atlanta: A Historical Time Line

1837   A surveyor's stake is placed in what is now Atlanta to mark the end, or terminus, of the Western and Atlantic Railroad

1843   The town of Terminus changes its name to Marthasville

1845   Marthasville becomes Atlanta

1861   Confederate President Jefferson Davis visits Atlanta; the Civil War begins

1864   Atlanta is the site of several major battles; the city surrenders to General Sherman, who orders it vacated and burned

1886   Coca-Cola is invented in Atlanta by John S. Pemberton

1895   The Cotton States and International Exposition is held at Piedmont Park

1929   Martin Luther King, Jr., is born in Atlanta

1936   *Gone with the Wind*, Atlantan Margaret Mitchell's best-selling Civil War novel, is published

1939   The world premiere of the film *Gone with the Wind* is held at the Loew's Grand Theatre in Atlanta

1960   Martin Luther King, Jr., leads a sit-in aimed at ending segregation of food service at a downtown Atlanta department store

1964   Martin Luther King, Jr., awarded Nobel Peace Prize

1971   Atlanta voters approve the beginning of the Metropolitan Atlanta Rapid Transit Authority (MARTA) rapid rail system.

1973   Maynard Jackson, Jr., the first black mayor of a major Southern city, is elected mayor of Atlanta

1976   George L. Smith II Georgia World Congress Center, a convention center, is completed

1986   Monday, January 20, 1986, marks the first national holiday honoring the birthday of Dr. Martin Luther King, Jr.

1988   Atlanta is chosen to represent the United States in the process of selecting the site of the 1996 Summer Olympic games; the Democratic National Convention is held in Atlanta to select the Democratic candidate for president of the United States

Index

Aaron, Henry, 44
Academy Theatre, 25, 51
Alliance Theatre, 25, 51
Ansley Park, 32
Appalachian Mountains, 12, 13-14
Atlanta: economy of, 15, 19, 20-23, 25-27; festivals of, 48-51; international activities of, 26-29, 31-32; names of, 19-20; nicknames of, 17; schools of, 23, 27, 32, 33; weather of, 12-13
Atlanta Ballet, 25
Atlanta Braves, 44
Atlanta Children's Theatre, 51
Atlanta Constitution, 20-22
Atlanta Cyclorama, 47
Atlanta Daily World, 36
Atlanta Falcons, 44
Atlanta-Fulton County Stadium, 44
Atlanta Opera, 50
Atlanta State Farmers Market, 47
Atlanta Symphony Orchestra, 25, 50, 51
Atlanta University Center, 23, 33
Auburn Avenue, 36-39, 48
Battle of Atlanta, 20, 47
Buckhead, 34-36
Cabbagetown, 33-34
Carter, Jimmy, 27
Carter Center, 27
Center for Puppetry Arts, 52

Centers for Disease Control (CDC), 26
Chattahoochee River, 42
Civil War, 11, 20, 29, 31
Coca-Cola, 22
Cotton States and International Exposition, 22
Davis, Jefferson, 45
Decatur, 42
Ebenezer Baptist Church, 39, 48
Fernbank Science Center, 42-44
Friendship Force, 27
Fulton County, 26
Georgia state capitol building, 13, 25-26
Gone with the Wind, 11
Governor's mansion, 36
Grady, Henry, 20-22
Grant Park, 47
Greek Orthodox Cathedral of the Annunciation, 48
Harris, Joel Chandler, 33
Hartsfield International Airport, 13, 26
High Museum of Art, 25
Inman Park, 34
International Cotton Exposition, 22
Jackson, Thomas "Stonewall," 45
King, Martin Luther, Jr., 33, 38-39
Lee, Robert E., 45
MARTA, 15
Marthasville, 19-20

Martin Luther King, Jr. National Historic Site
   and Preservation District, 38-39, 48
Mitchell, Margaret, 11
New Georgia Railroad, 47
New South movement, 22
Peachtree, as name, 14-15, 17
Peachtree Junior, 42
Peachtree Road Race, 41-42
Pemberton, John S., 22
Phoenix, 29
Piedmont Exhibition, 22
Piedmont Park, 15, 32, 41, 48, 50
Piedmont Plateau, 12
Royal Peacock, 36

Shaw, Robert, 25
Sherman, William T., 20
Southern Center for International Studies, 27
Stone Mountain, 13, 45
Stone Mountain Park, 44-47, 48
Summer Olympic Games, 27-29
Sweet Auburn. *See* Auburn Avenue
Symphony Hall, 51
Terminus, 19, 32
West End, 32-33
Western and Atlantic Railroad, 19
Westin Peachtree Plaza Hotel, 13, 14
Woodruff Arts Center, 49, 51
Wren's Nest, 33